Mysterious Mazes

Christian Kämpf

Sterling Publishing Co., Inc.
New York

Library of Congress Cataloging-in-Publication Data
Available

10   9   8   7   6   5   4   3   2   1

Published in 2003 by Sterling Publishing Co., Inc.
387 Park Avenue South
New York, NY 10016
First published in Germany under the title *Geheimnisvolle*
Labyrinthe by Edition Bücherbär im Arena Verlag GmbH
Wurzburg, Germany
© 2001 Edition Büchorbär im Arona Vorlag GmbH
English Translation© 2003 by Sterling Publishing Co., Inc.
Distributed in Canada by Sterling Publishing
C/o Canadian Manda Group, One Atlantic Avenue, Suite 105
Toronto, Ontario, M6K 3E7, Canada
Distributed in Great Britain by Chris Lloyd at Orca Book
Services, Stanley House, Fleets Lane, Poole BH15 3AJ, England
Distributed in Australia by Capricorn Link (Australia) Pty Ltd.
P.O. Box 704, Windsor, NSW 2756, Australia

Printed in China
All Rights Reserved

Sterling ISBN 1-4027-0297-3

Freddy the Fox is a genius when it comes to finding his way through mazes. He can help you find hidden treasures, secret passageways, and buried objects. Good luck—you're going to need it!

This small caterpillar is trying to reach Freddy. Can you help her find the shortest way to him?

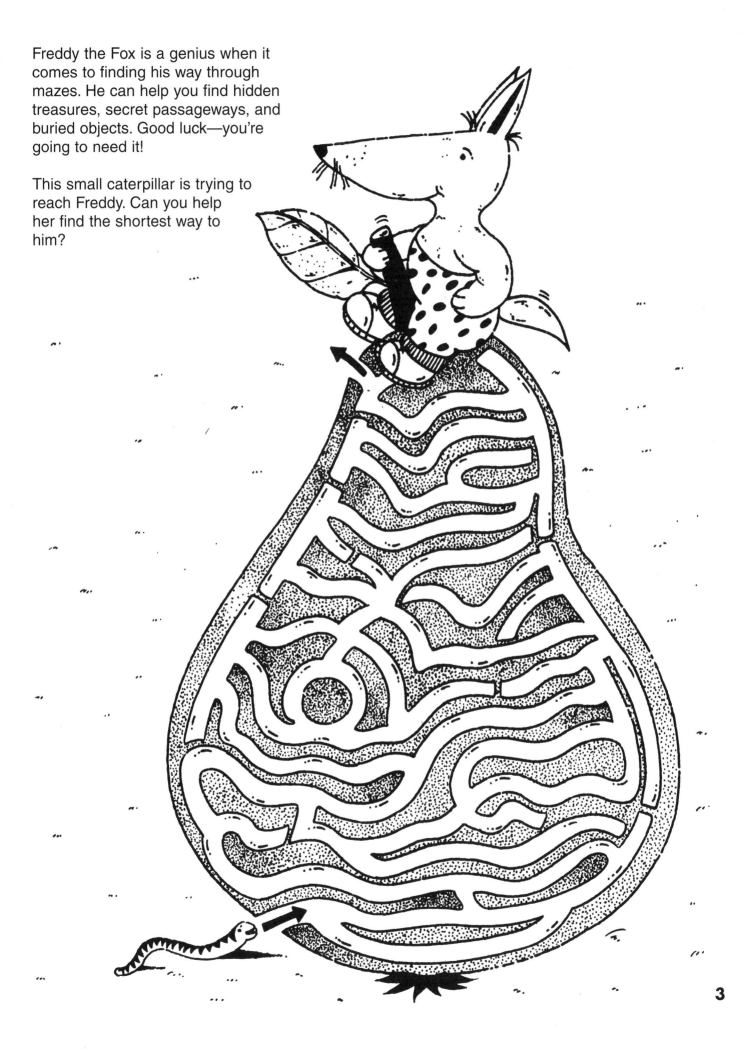

Thirsty Pirates

Freddy is trying to bring his friends a barrel of water for their long journey home on the sea. Unfortunately, the rope ladder has holes all over it. Help Freddy follow the rope to find his thirsty friends.

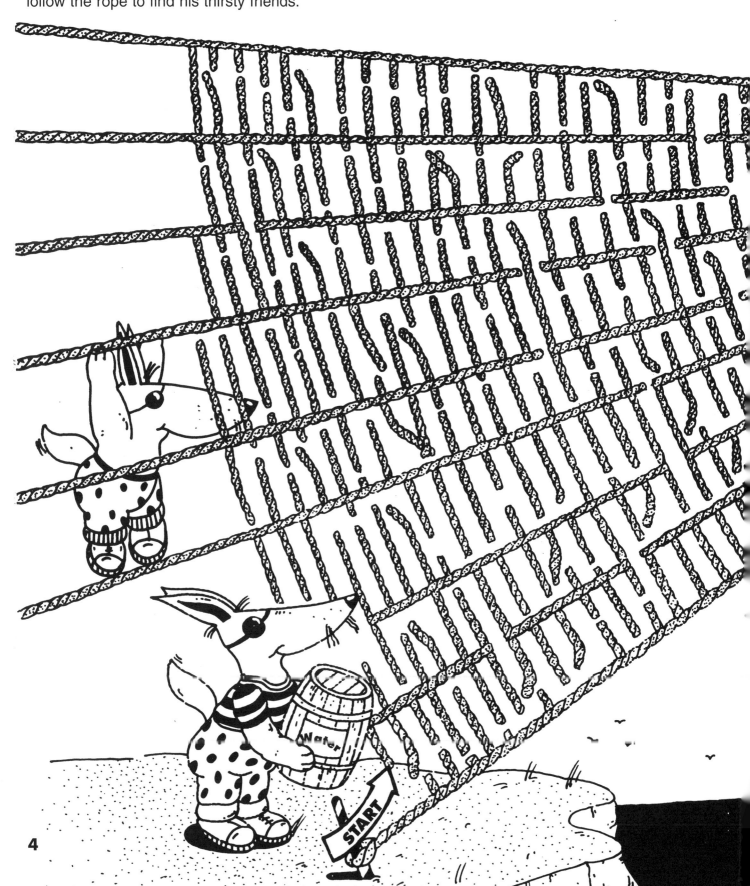

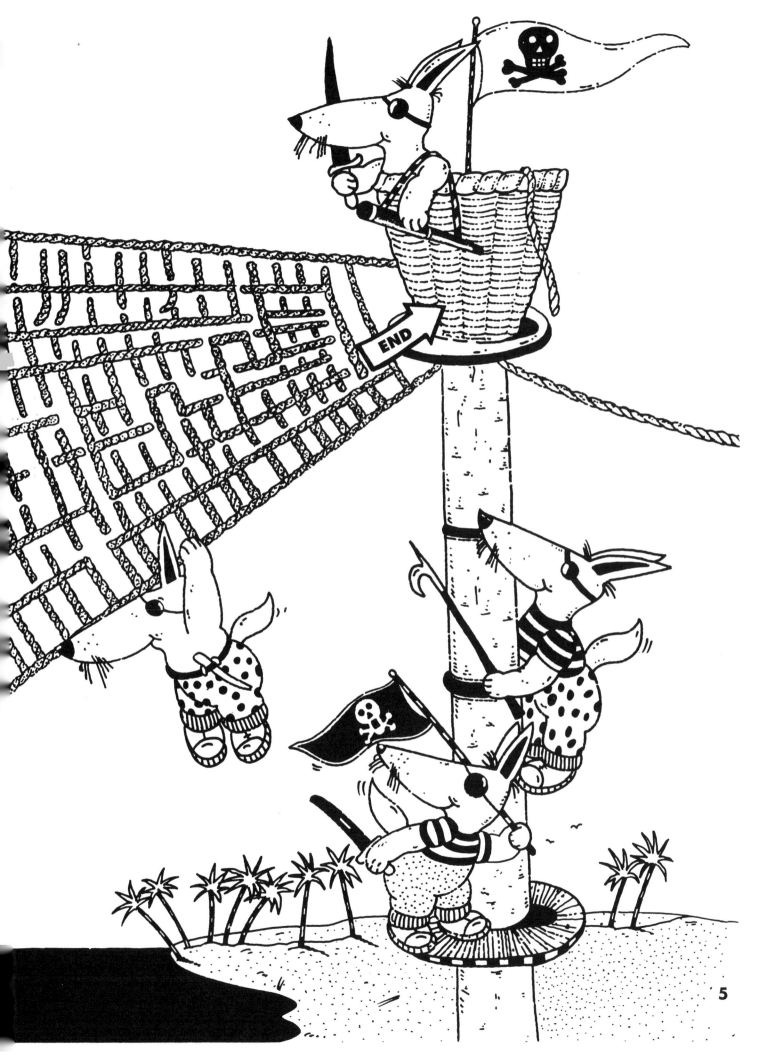

END

5

Tangled Thread

Freddy and his friends need to sew some clothes.
Whose thread will get them to the thimble?

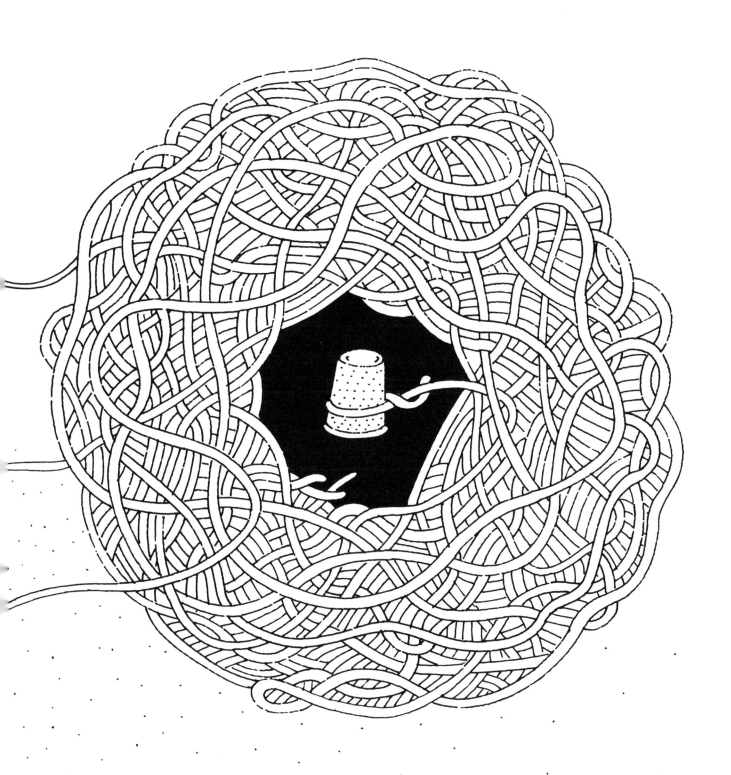

A Hot Summer Day

Which straw is in the lemonade?

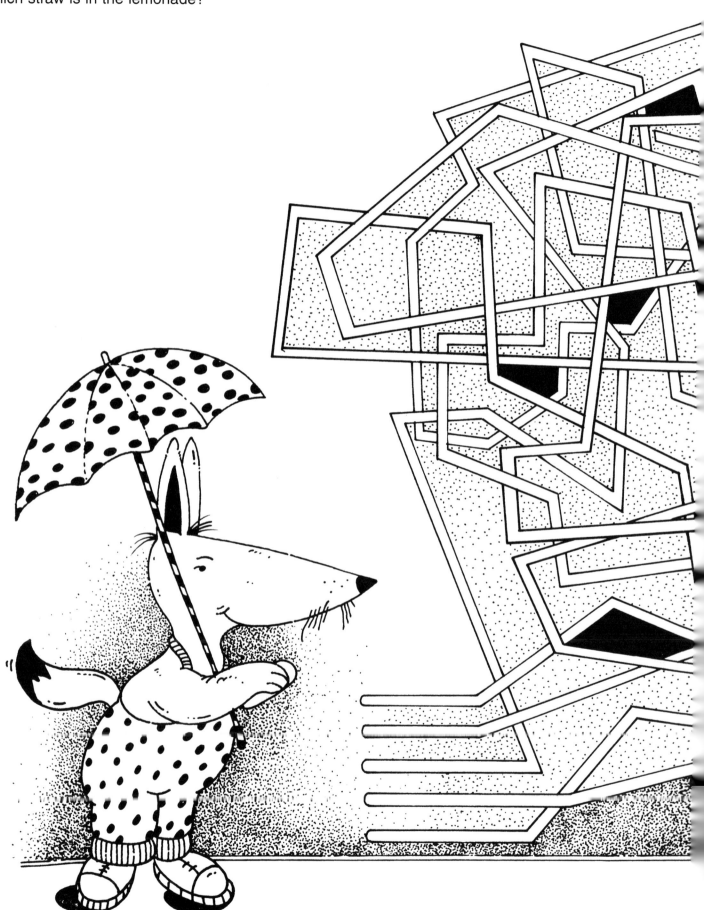

8

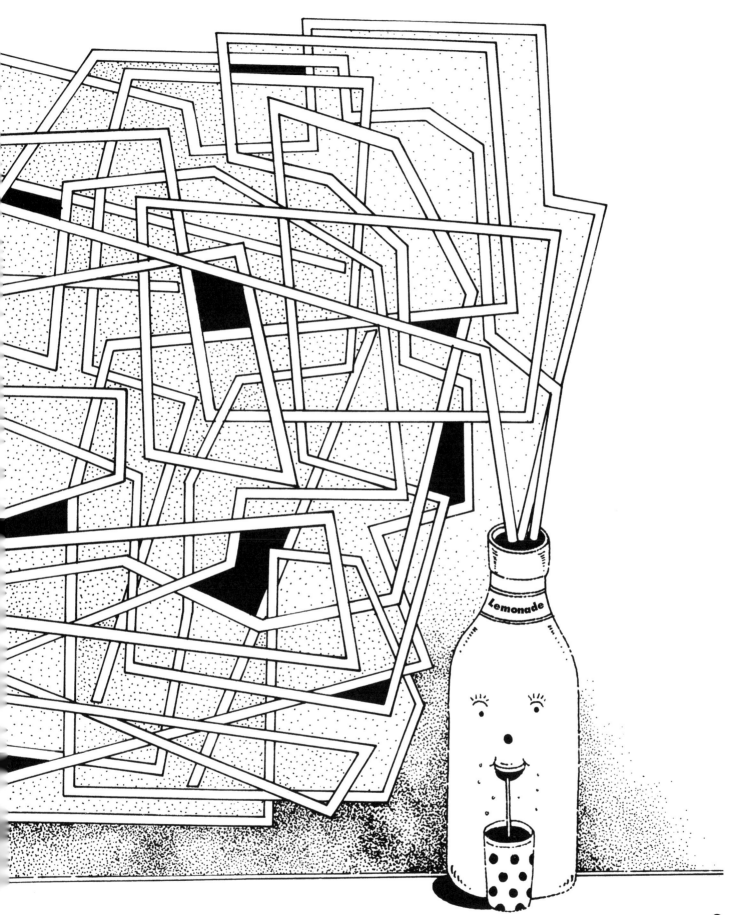

Lemonade

Smiling Faces

The correct path to the laughing face in the upper right-hand corner can only be reached by going from one smiling face to the next. Can you do it?

START

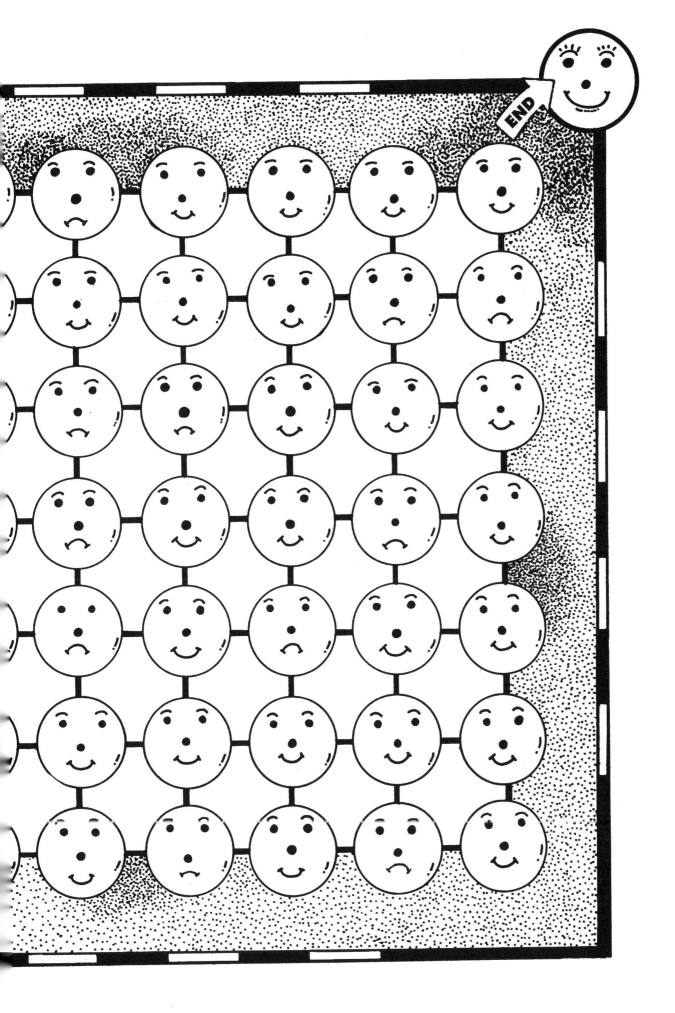

END

11

Swimming Ducks

Follow the strings to see which one is attached to a rubber duck.

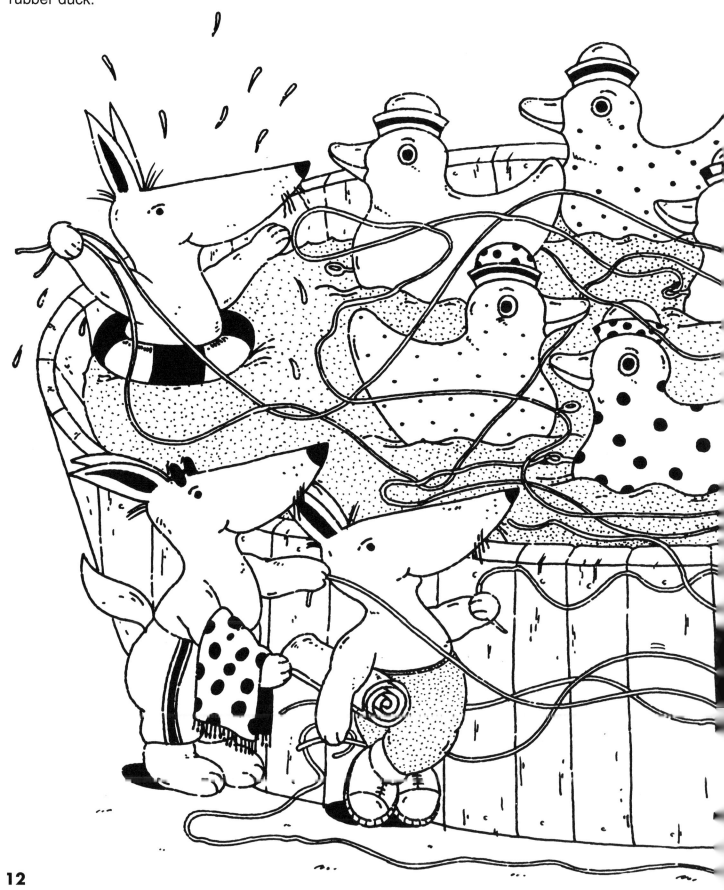

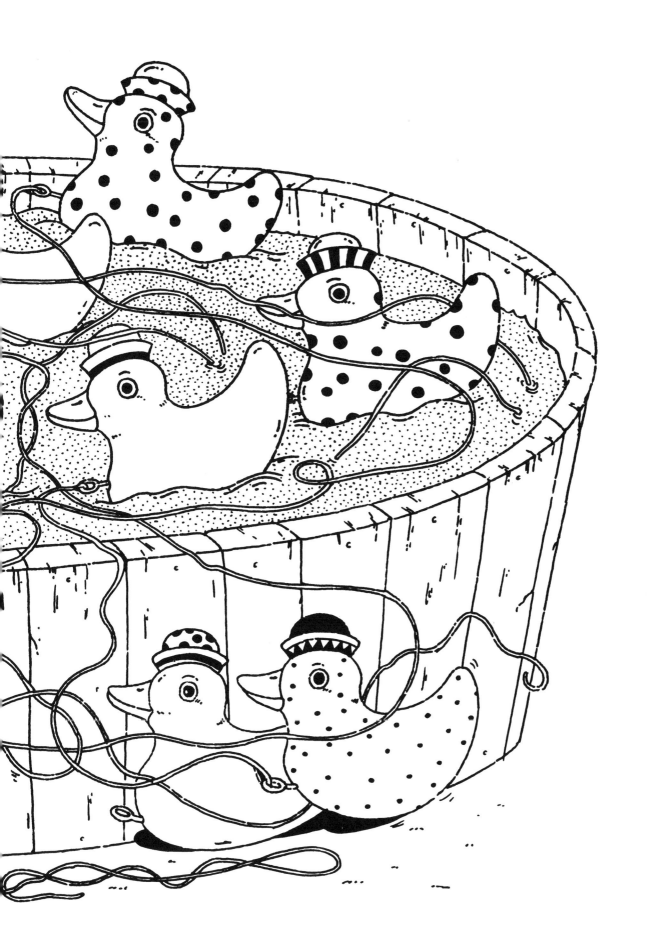

The City of Pyramids

How can Freddy reach the Moon Pyramid?

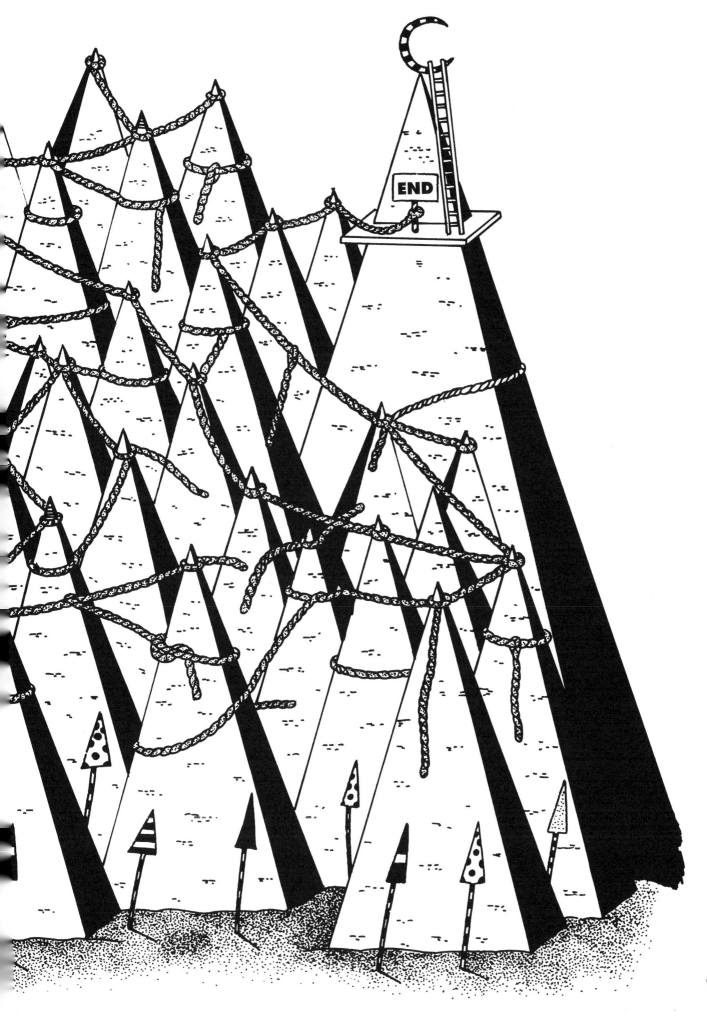

The Gobi Desert

Freddy and his friends can't take the heat of the Gobi Desert anymore! Can you help them get the bottle of soda?

The Mayan Pyramid

Freddy is on an expedition to study the ancient Mayan pyramids. At the top of the pyramid is the famous Golden Idol. What's the best way to go?

START

Tricky Dice

To get to the end of this maze you can only follow
the dice in this order: 1, 2, 3, 4, 5, 6. Then start with
1 again and repeat the order. Can you do it?

START

Rollerblade Race

Start with the lines from each fox's rollerblades and see which one leads to the lemonade stand.

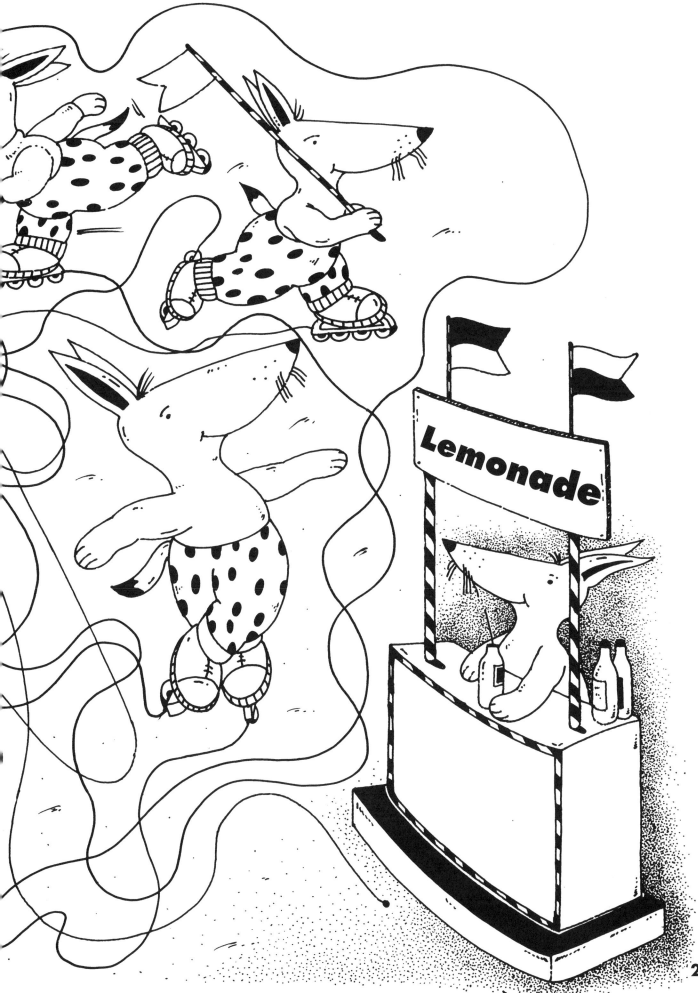

Lemonade

Floating Rafts

Freddy is trying to reach the raft with the palm tree and glass of soda. Which way does he have to go?

Fields of Pollen

Freddy is collecting pollen for a science experiment. But in order to reach the pile of pollen, he can only move from a black to a white flower petal or piece of stem each time. Can you help guide him?

26

27

Catching Butterflies

Freddy wants to catch a butterfly only to look at; then he'll let it go. The one he really wants is flying by itself. The others are all connected. Can you figure out which butterfly each one is connected to and which one is flying free?

The Toucan Ride

How can Freddy reach his friends so that he can enjoy the toucan ride with them?

Flower Mill

Freddy is helping his friends grind wheat to make flour. Only one path will carry the grain from the top to bottom. Which one?

Grain

Flour

33

Freddy's Hut

Freddy is visiting a tropical island and is lost. Can you direct him to his hut?

START

END

Tangled Balloons

How many balloons are attached to the strings? Start at the balloons and wind your way down.

Adding Numbers

In order to get to the end, Freddy has to cross over the numbers and add them up. Which way does he have to go in order to arrive at the sum of 53?

The Egyptian Stone

The Egyptian Stone has twenty-eight corners. How can you reach the center?

38

Trapped!

Freddy got himself trapped in the maze! In order to get out, he has to add numbers together to obtain the sum of 35. Which way should he go?

The Maze Diagram

Can you get to the middle of the maze?

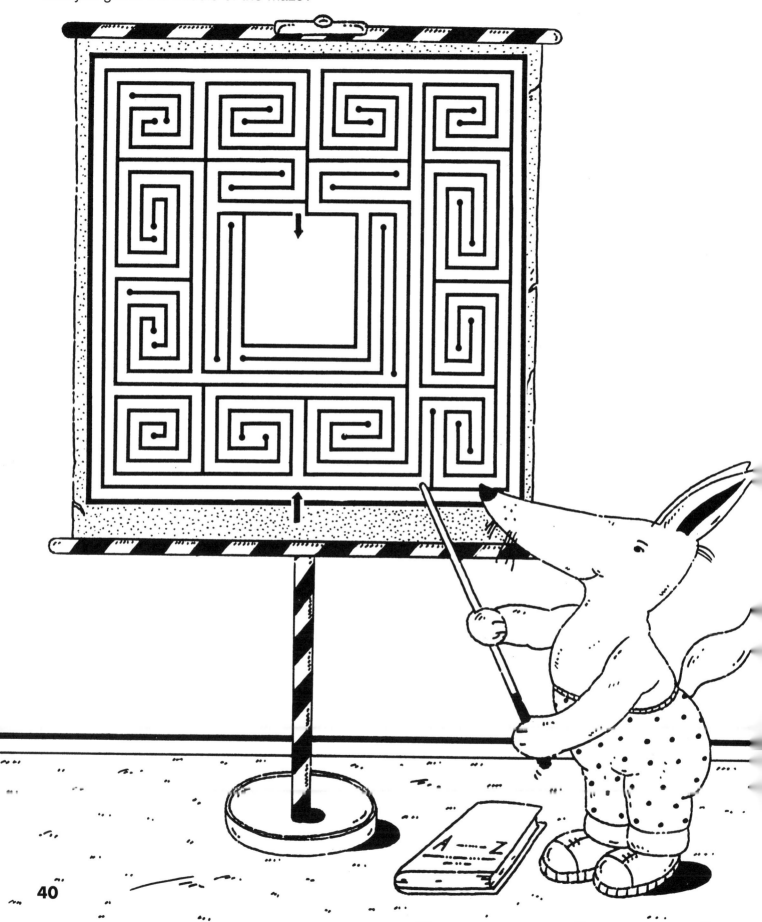

The Stone Wheel

Freddy has discovered the Stone Wheel. But how can he get to the center?

Balloon Fun

Which balloon is Freddy holding?

The Star Balloon

How can you reach the balloon's center?

Flying Freddy

Can you figure out which kites are attached to the plane, which ones are not, and which kites are linked together?

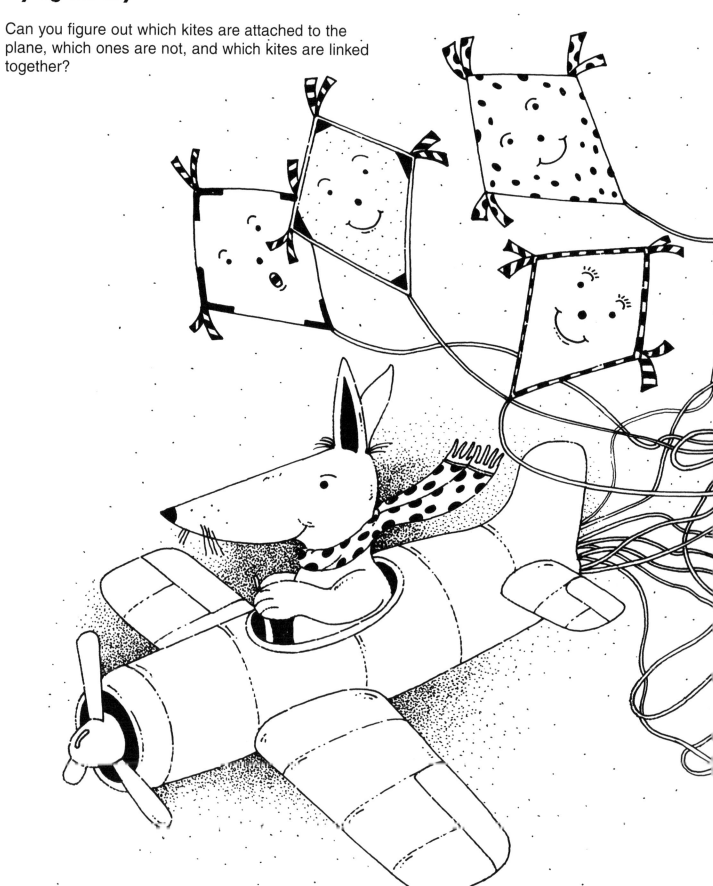

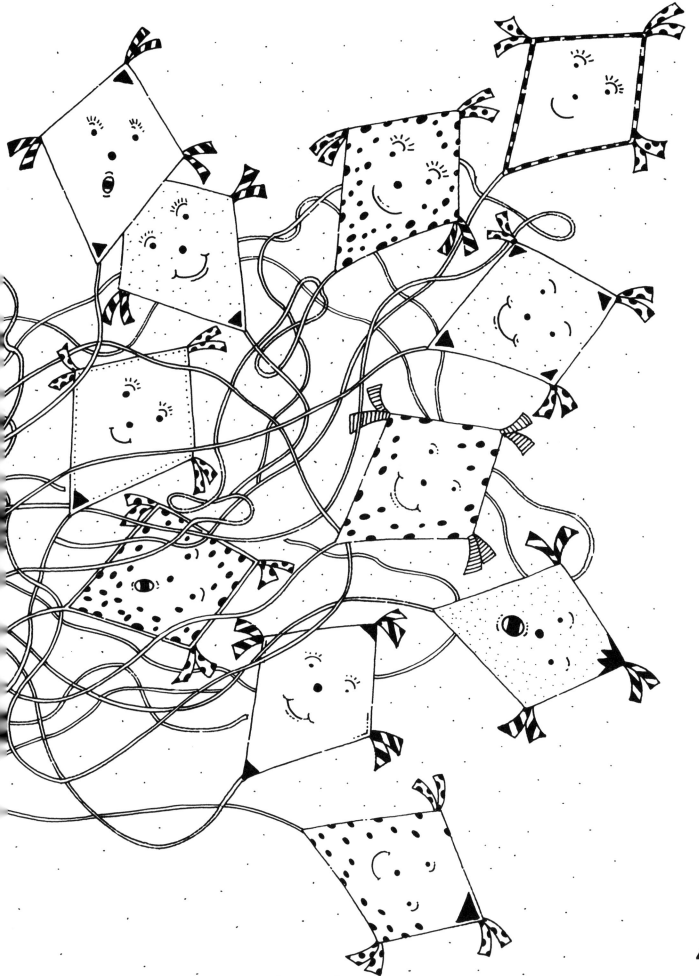

Worm Race

Which path should the worm take to reach the end of the maze?

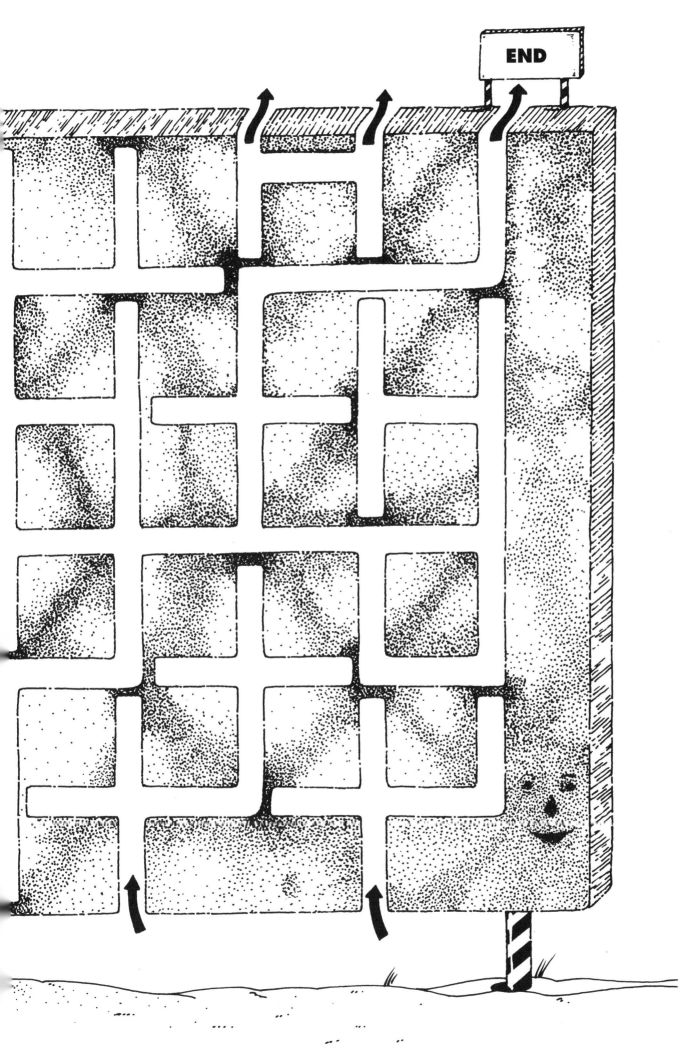

END

Spaghetti Dinner

Freddy is preparing a great-tasting spaghetti dinner for his friend Bob. But, before Bob can eat it, he has to collect the items that Freddy is missing. He needs to get one plate, one spoon, one fork, one cup, one napkin, one bottle of ketchup, one salt shaker, and one bottle of soda. Can you get through the maze in this order?

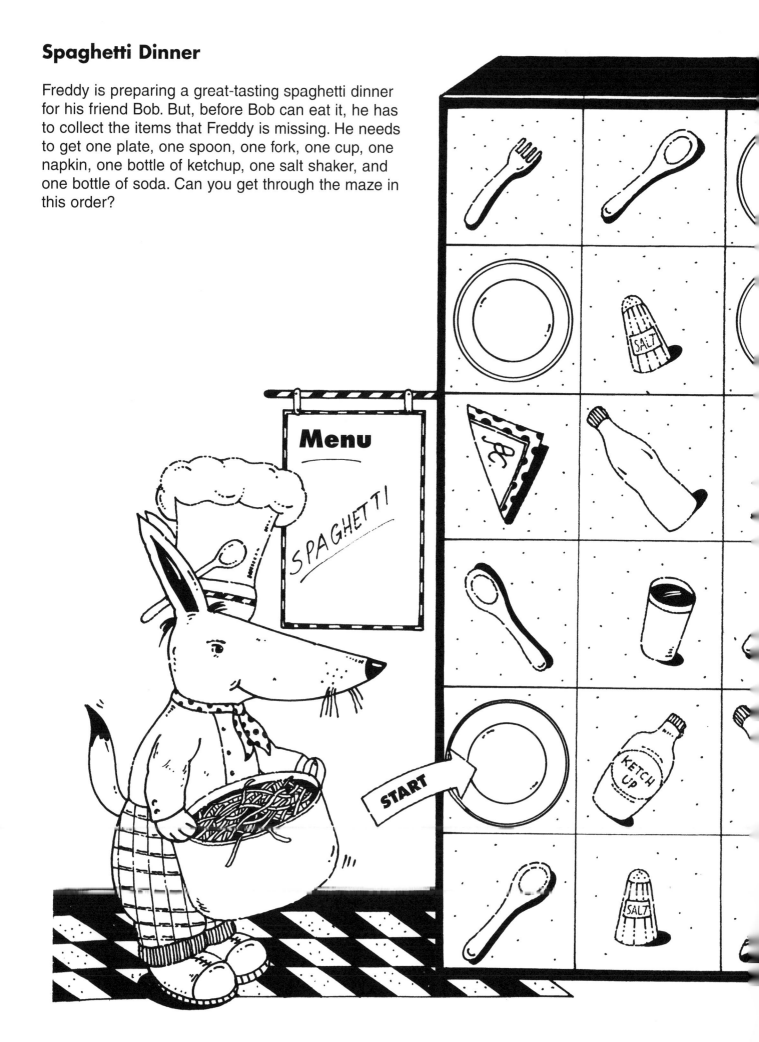

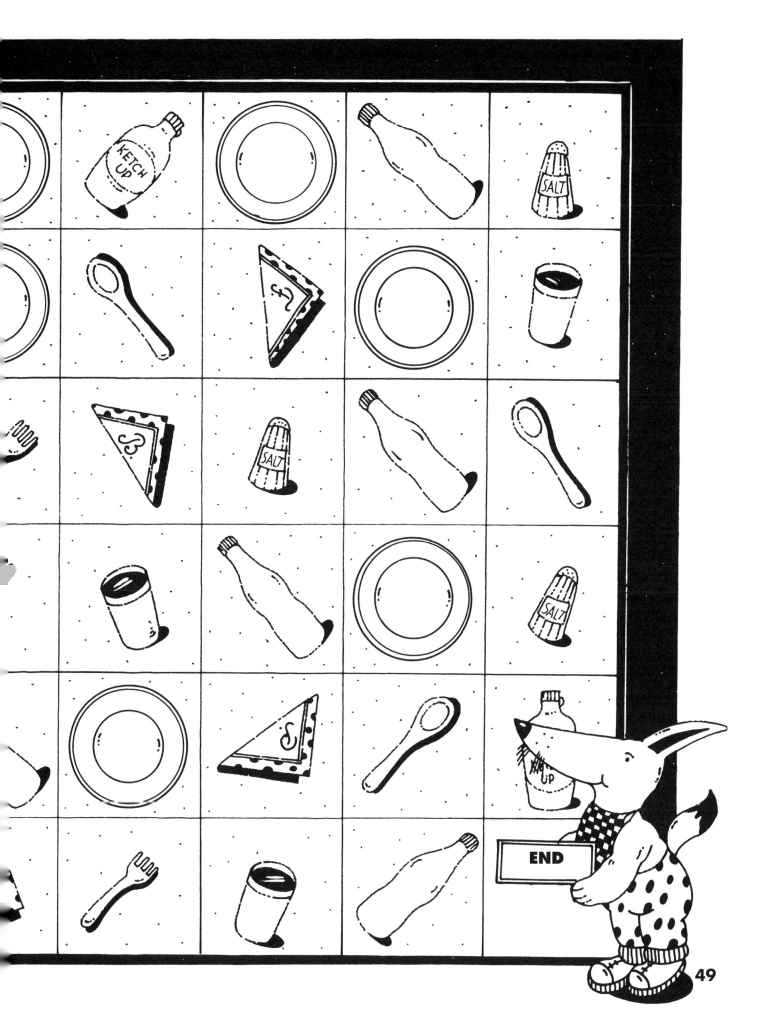

END

Pirate's Treasure

How can Freddy and his friends reach the treasure of gold?

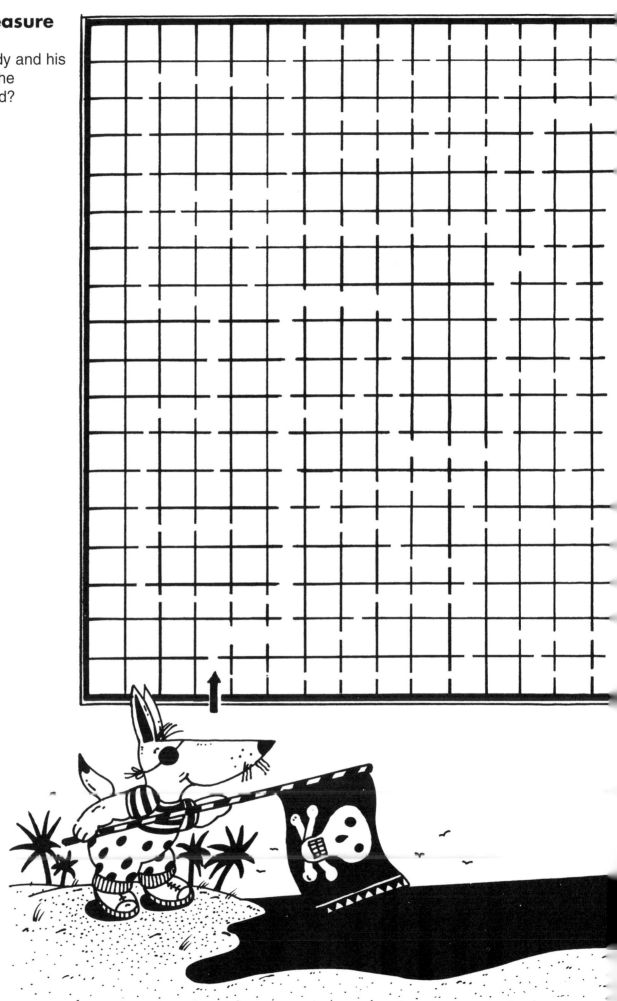

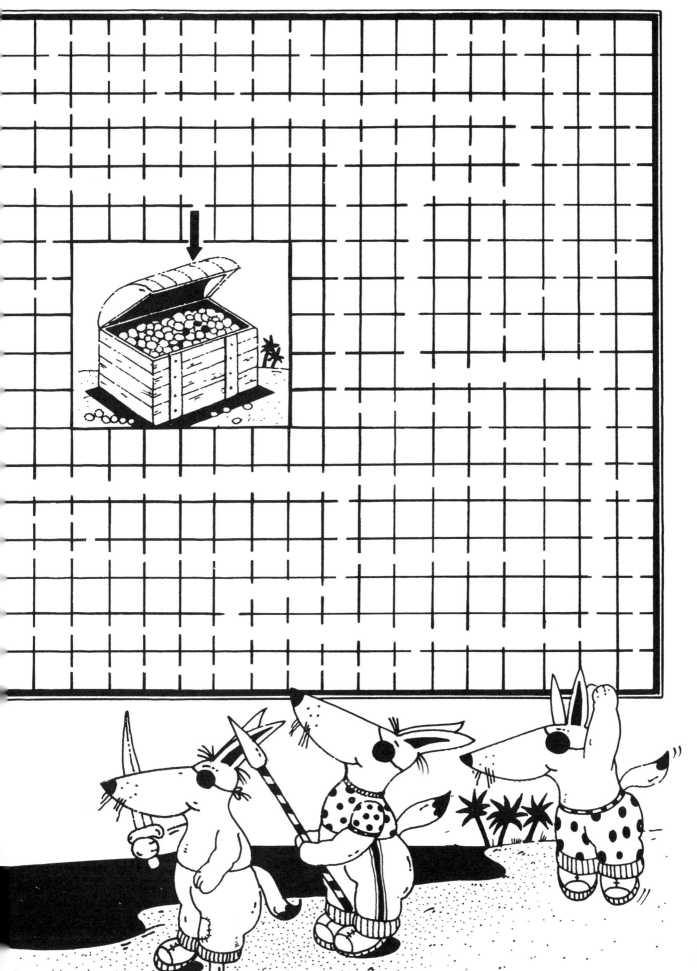

Koko

Freddy's pet parrot Koko got out of her cage. Can you help him catch her? Which ladder isn't broken?

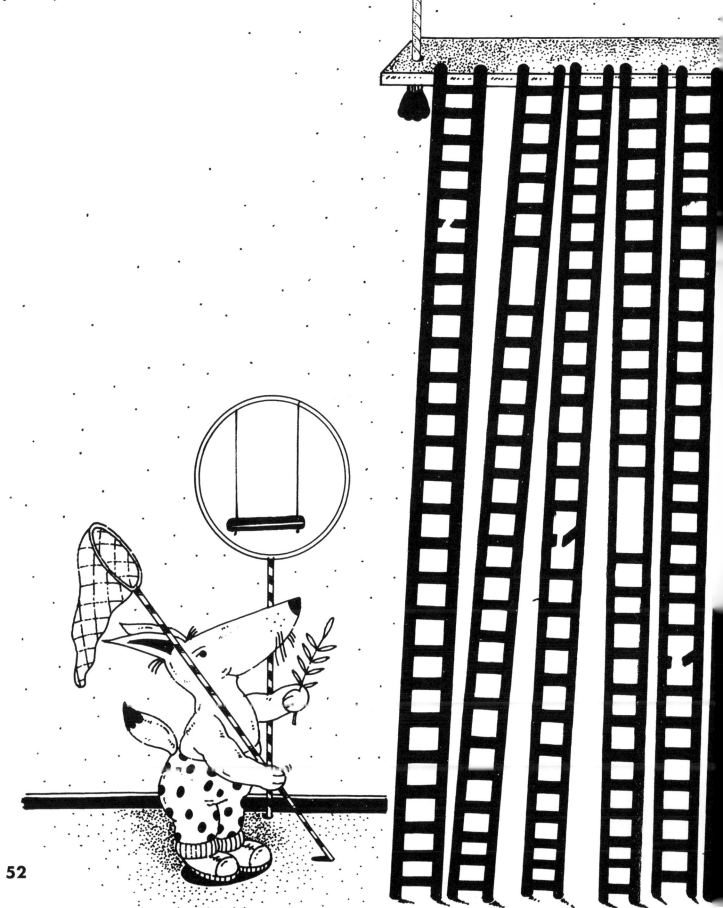

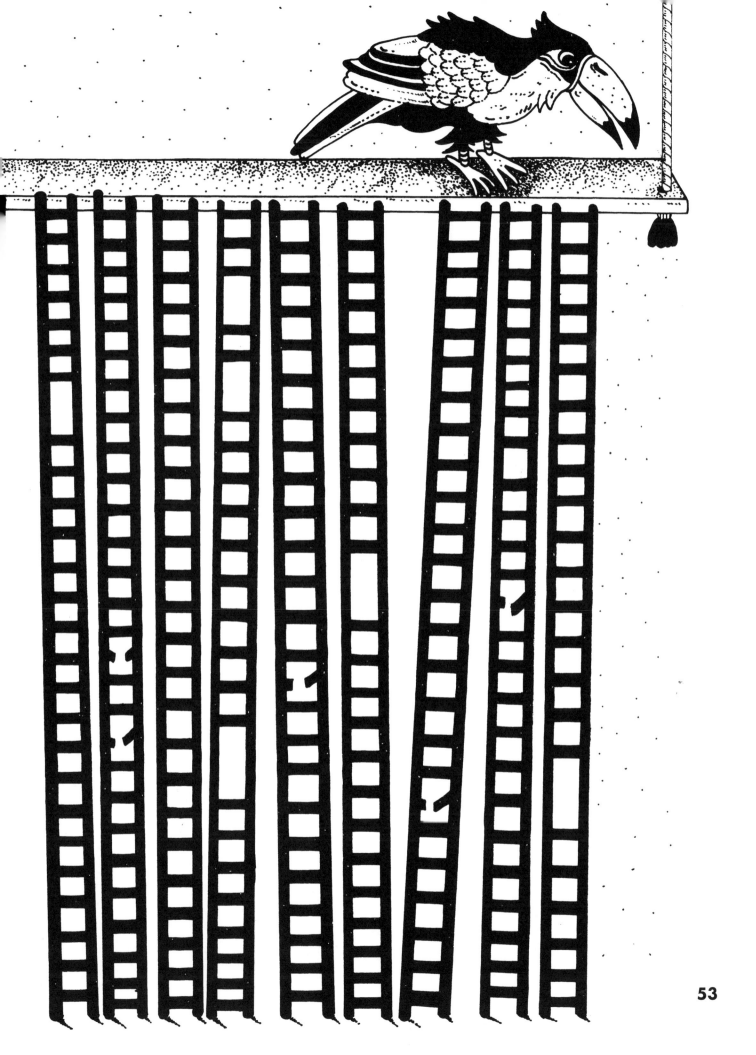

Sleeping Sam

Freddy and his friend Sam are supposed to go to the movies, but Sam is still sleeping! Now they are running late! Can you help Freddy find Sam and wake him up? Make sure Freddy avoids the earthworms.

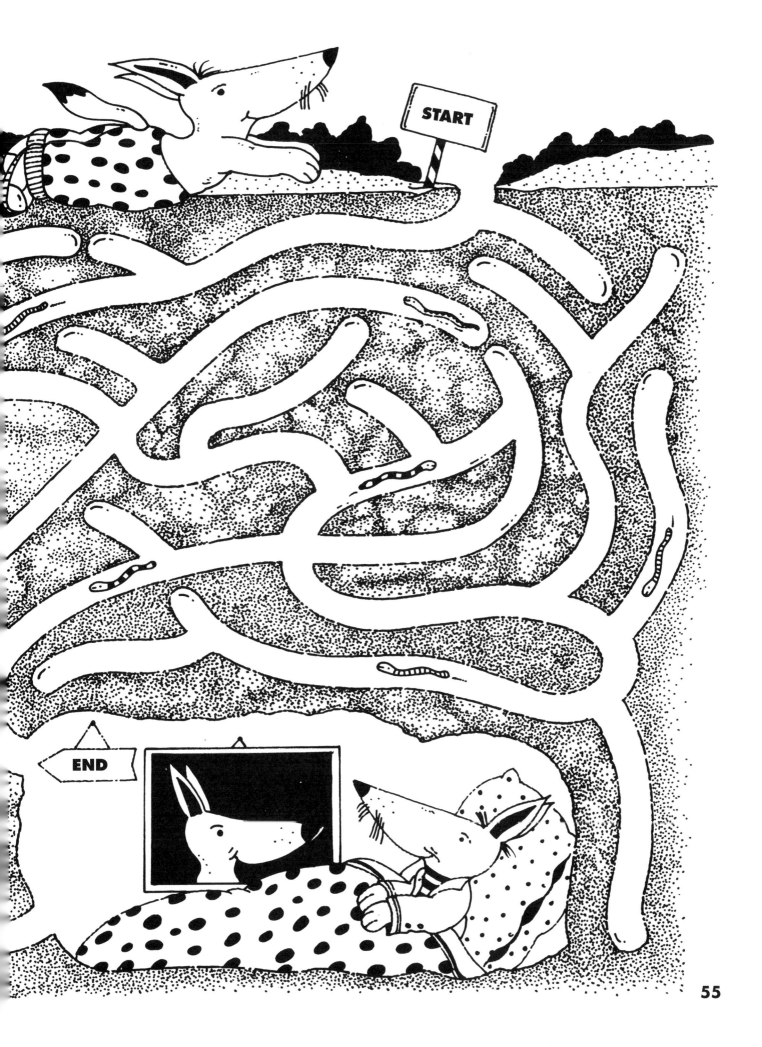

START

END

The Double Pyramids

Help Freddy get through the left pyramid and then the right pyramid. Which path will you start with?

START

END

Chemistry Lab

Through which tubes does the liquid have to travel in order to reach the main compound?

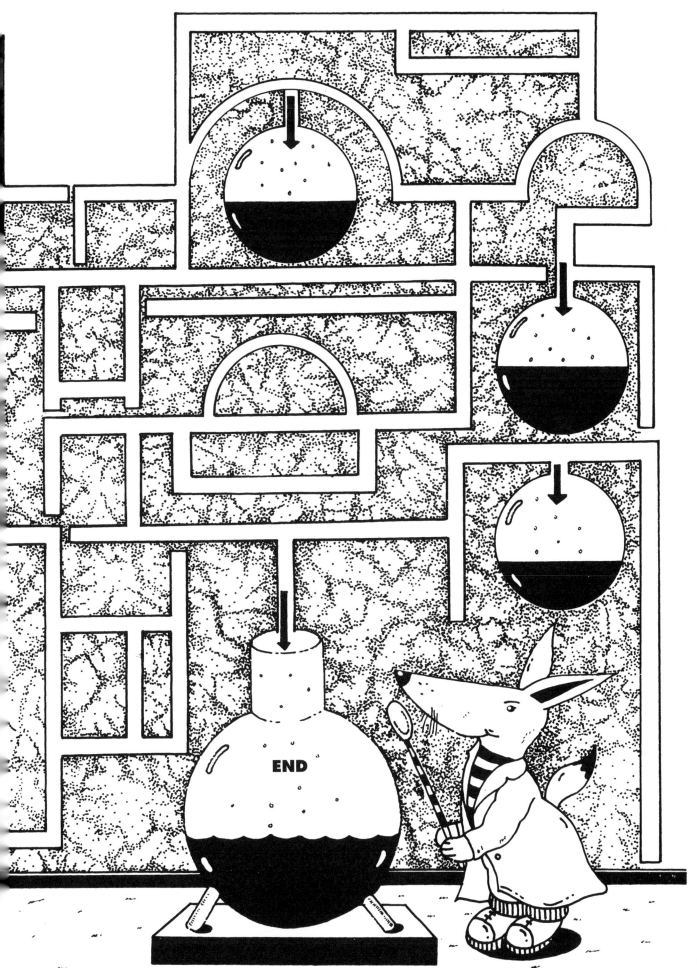

A Balloon Mix-up

Which fox has 3 of the same kind of balloons. Start with the string in each one's hand.

Party Hat

How can you get through this party hat?

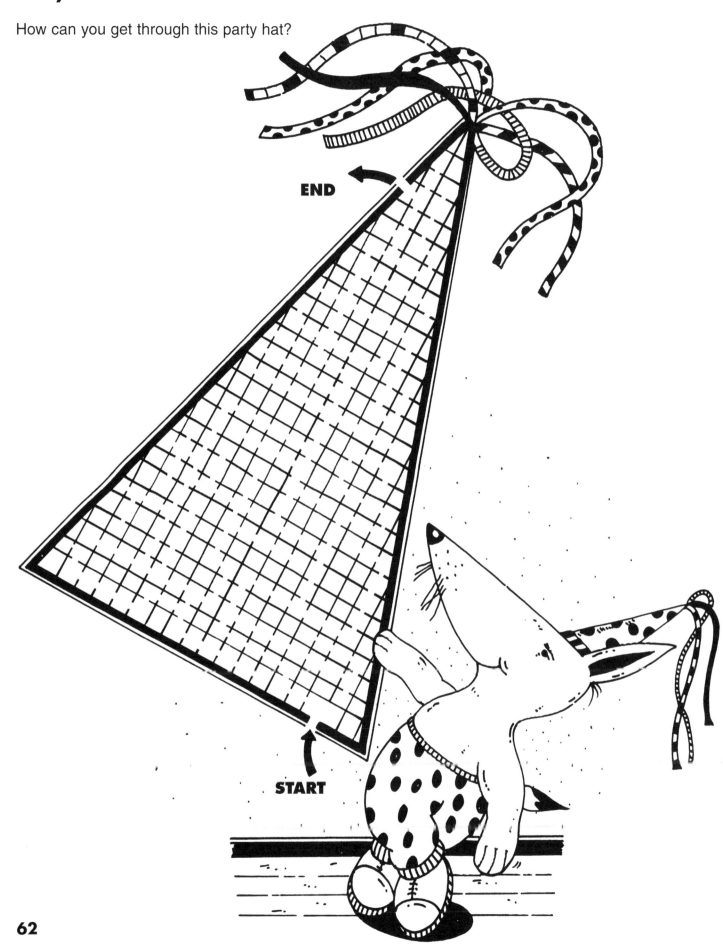

END

START

The Computer Maze

Freddy's computer is broken. Can you help him find
the center in order to fix it?

Fishing with Freddy

Which fish has Freddy caught?

One Thousand and One Ladders

Only through a secret passage among ladders can
Freddy reach the Great Star Palace. Can you find it?

START

END

Number Desert

Which path of numbers adds up to 76?

Grassy Paths

Freddy made a bunch of paths while mowing his lawn. Now he is lost and cannot find his way back to the shed. Can you help him?

The Ancient Stone Head

There is only one way through the maze to the stone head of a Mayan prince. Can you find it?

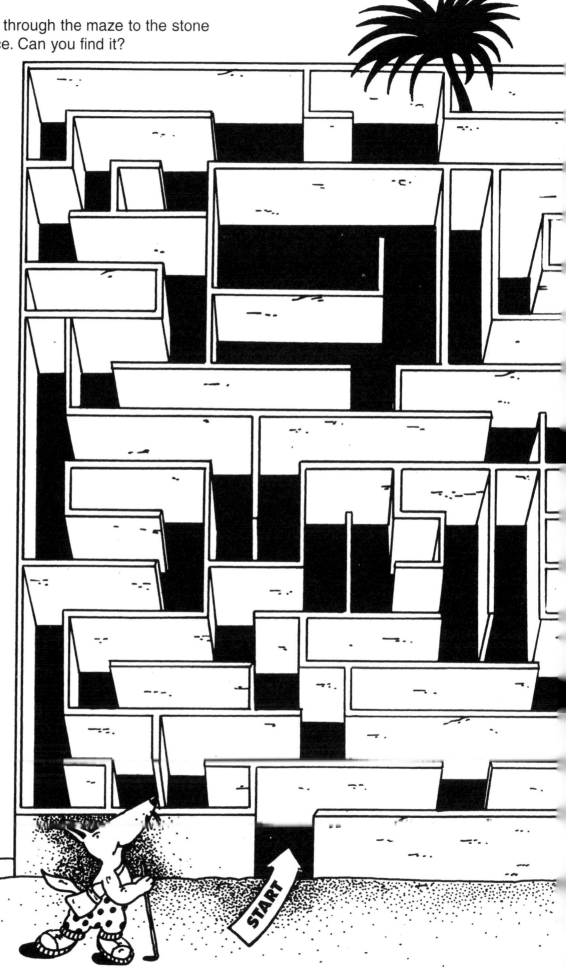

START

The Tiger Pyramid

Which way up or down the ladders can Freddy reach the tiger's head?

Confused Divers

Which fox is actually attached to the oxygen tank?

Marble Track

Which path does the marble have to take in order to
reach the clown's mouth?

END

Telephone Chaos

To whom is Freddy talking?

Two of a Kind

If Freddy follows the correct domino trail, he will reach the end; but he needs your help! He can only go through the dominoes that have a matching pair of symbols.

START

Medieval Town

How can Freddy reach the castle?
Start at the front gate.

Tutan-Fox's Mummy

Freddy is trying to find the lost tomb of Tutan-Fox.
Can you find it?

Maze Painting

Freddy is admiring the Maze Painting. He can't help
but wonder how to get to the center of it! Can you?

Answers

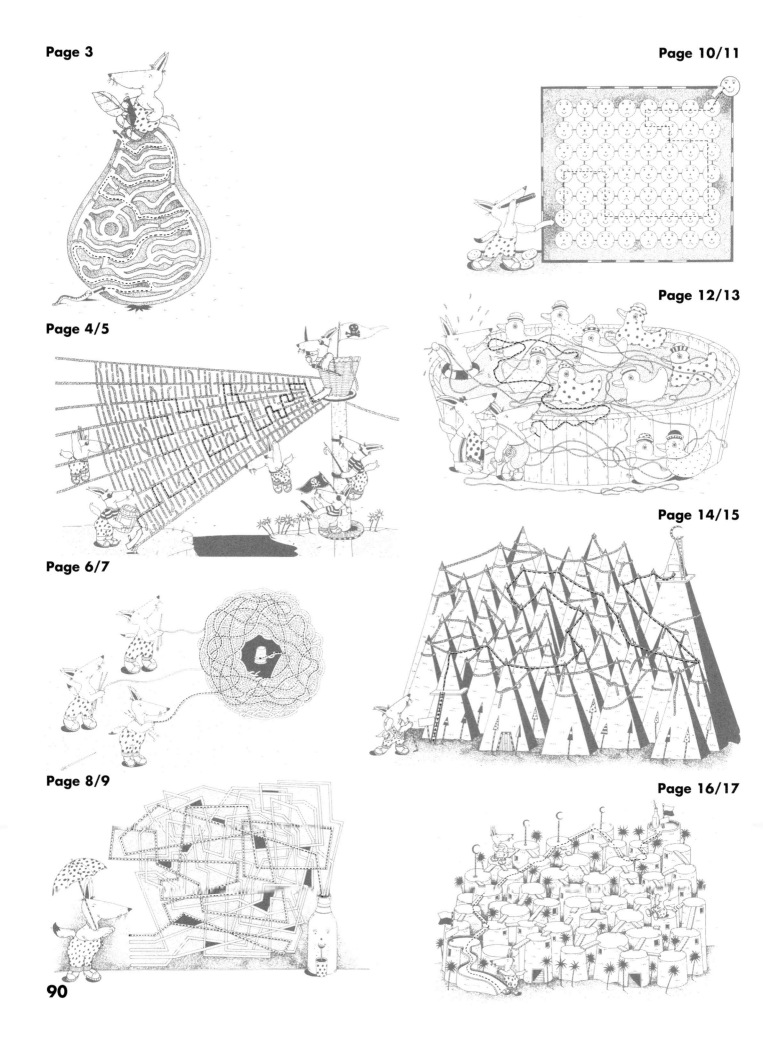

Page 3

Page 10/11

Page 4/5

Page 12/13

Page 6/7

Page 14/15

Page 8/9

Page 16/17

Page 18/19

Page 26/27

Page 20/21

Page 28/29

A-K, B-G, C-D, E-I, F-M, N-O, J-L

Page 22/23

Friend A

Page 30/31

Page 24/25

Page 32/33

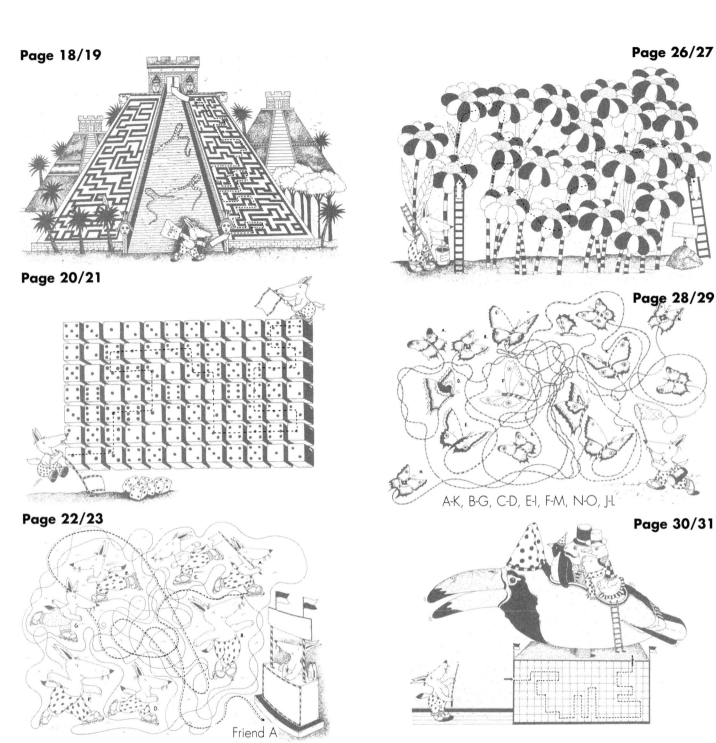

Page 34/35

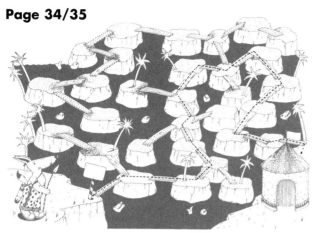

Page 39

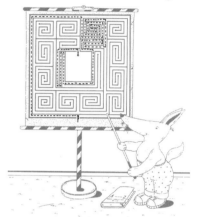

Page 36

2 Balloons

Page 40

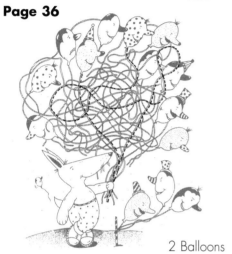

Page 37

Page 41

Page 38

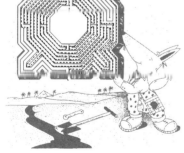

92

Page 42/43

The pig

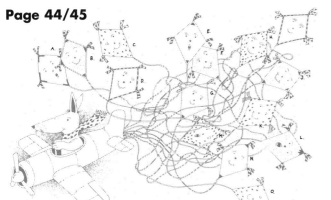

L/E/O/N/J are attached to airplane. A/B/D/F/G/I are not attached. C is linked to K. H is linked to M

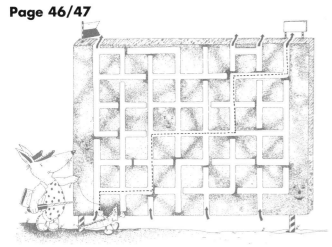

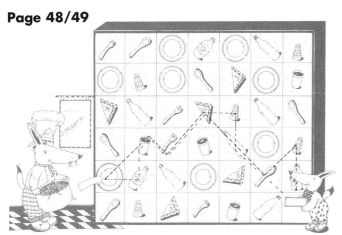

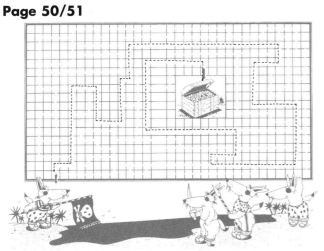

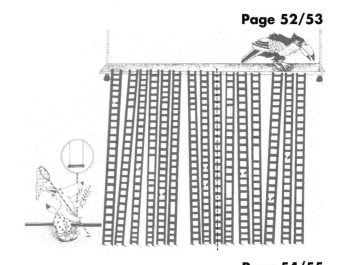

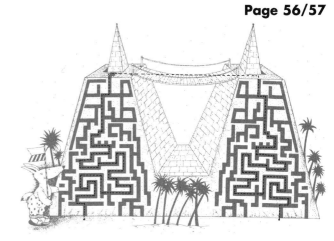

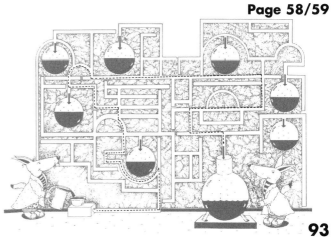

Page 60/61

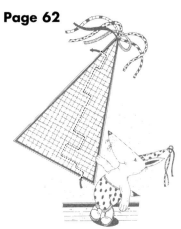

Page 66/67

Page 62

Page 68/69

15+3+1+5+1+10+5+7+19+5=76

Page 63

Page 70/71

Page 64/65

Page 72/73

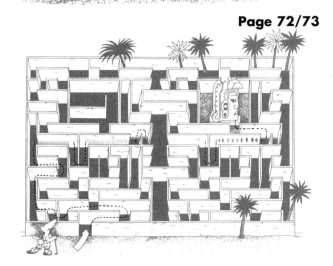

Page 74/75

Page 82/83

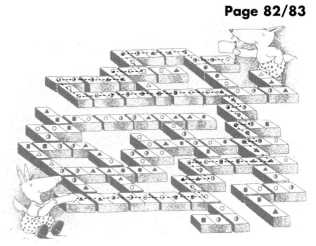

Page 76/77

Page 84/85

Page 78/79

Page 86/87

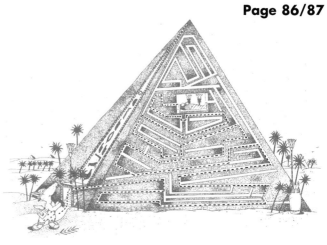

Page 88

Page 80/81

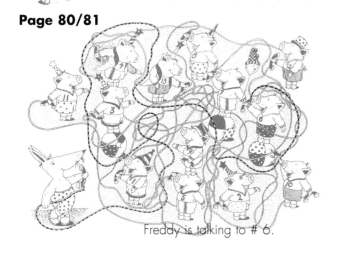

Freddy is talking to # 6.

95

Index